The New Novello Choral Edition

JOHANN SEBASTIAN BACH

Magnificat in D (ʙᴡᴠ243)

Magnificat in E flat (ʙᴡᴠ243a)

for solo voices, SATB choir and orchestra

Vocal score

Edited, with a new translation of the four Lauds,
by Neil Jenkins

Order No: NOV 072529

NOVELLO PUBLISHING LIMITED

It is requested that on all concert notices and programmes acknowledgement is made to 'The New Novello Choral Edition'.

Es wird gebeten, auf sämtlichen Konzertankündigungen und Programmen 'The New Novello Choral Edition' als Quelle zu erwähnen.

Il est exigé que toutes notices et programmes de concerts, comportent des remerciements à 'The New Novello Choral Edition'.

Orchestral material is available on hire from the Publisher.

Orchestermaterial ist beim Verlag erhältlich.

Les partitions d'orchestre sont en location disponibles chez l'editeur.

Permission to reproduce from the Preface of this Edition must be obtained from the Publisher.

Die Erlaubnis, das Vorwort dieser Ausgabe oder Teile desselben zu reproduzieren, muß beim Verlag eingeholt werden.

Le droit de reproduction de ce document à partir de la préface doit être obtenu de l'éditeur.

Cover illustration: facsimile of the first page of the original score of Bach's *Magnificat* in D. Reproduced by permission of the Berlin State Library (Music Department with Mendelssohn Archive) [Mus. ms. Bach P39, 1. Notenseite]

© 2000 Novello & Company Limited

Published in Great Britain by Novello Publishing Limited
Head Office: 14-15 Berners Street, London W1T 3LJ
Tel +44 (0)20 7612 7400   Fax +44 (0)20 7612 7546

Sales and Hire: Music Sales Distribution Centre
Newmarket Road, Bury St Edmunds, Suffolk IP33 3YB
Tel +44 (0)1284 702600   Fax +44 (0)1284 768301

Web: www.musicsales.com   e-mail: music@musicsales.co.uk

All rights reserved   Printed in Great Britain

Music setting by Stave Origination

CONTENTS

PREFACE

Magnificat in E flat (BWV243a)

Magnificat in D has long been regarded as one of Bach's finest short choral works and is frequently performed on festive occasions. Far less well known, though undeservedly so, is the setting of the Magnificat on which *Magnificat* in D is based: *Magnificat* in E flat composed in 1723, Bach's first year as Kantor at the Thomaskirche in Leipzig. This may explain the fact that Bach's obituary (the *Neokrolog*) written jointly by J. F. Agricola (a former pupil and amanuensis) and C.P.E. Bach (his second son) specifically mentions his list of compositions as including 'many Oratorios, Masses and Magnificats'. According to Robert L. Marshall[1], Bach had the luxury of almost six weeks in which to prepare this work together with a setting of the Sanctus, BWV238, and a revision of Cantata BWV63 for performance on Christmas Day, 1723. Consisting of twelve movements, and with four inserted pieces - the Laudes or Lauds not belonging to this portion of St. Luke's Gospel - *Magnificat*, despite the brevity of its arias, is double the length of his normal weekly cantatas and, as such, the work provided the new Kantor with the means of impressing his new employers and congregation. Moreover, it contains many more elaborate choruses than were required of the weekly cantatas, and no *secco* recitatives or four-part chorales, which would have been quick and easy to compose.

Its structure and tonal scheme are satisfyingly symmetric and have long been admired by scholars. The choruses are followed by three groups of solo movements in related keys, the last of which is always for an increased number of singers (thus No. 3 is a solo, No. 6 is a duet and No. 10 is a trio.) So as to break up an otherwise long sequence of arias, the chorus returns in No. 4 to sing two appropriate words detached from the previous aria : 'omnes generationes' ('all generations'). C.S. Terry noted[2] that a similar device had been used in a *Magnificat* in G minor attributed to Albinoni. But Bach was able to take this simple idea and craft it into twenty seven bars of majestic counterpoint leading to a splendid climax on a chord of a dominant minor ninth at bar 24. In what was then a bold gesture, this chord is left unresolved, though this was not the case in the later revision. No.10 employs the *tonus peregrinus*, to which the Magnificat was traditionally chanted, as an instrumental counterpoint to the voices; in the first version, this is given to a solo trumpet, and in the revision to unison oboes.

In the following movement ('Sicut locutus est') a reference to 'our forefathers, Abraham and his seed' inspires Bach to look back at the music of his predecessors in Leipzig, such as Johann Kuhnau (1660-1722) whom he had so recently succeeded. Consequently, the music is written in an old fashioned *a cappella* fugal style that would have been familiar to earlier congregations. The lesser doxology 'Gloria Patri et Filio' brings the work back to its home key; and at the words 'sicut erat in principio' ('as it was in the beginning'), Bach enjoys one of his musical jokes by reintroducing the music of the work's opening bars. Although this device was not unknown to composers of the Baroque, its appropriateness at this point would have appealed to Bach. The composition is full of such delightful word painting: 'dispersit' is vigorously 'scattered'; 'exaltavit' and 'deposuit' graphically depict 'rising' and 'falling'; and, in the closing bars of No. 6, the words 'timentibus eum' ('them that fear him') are sung to a plangent repeated note (particularly at bar 31) which suggests intensely controlled nervousness.

The Four Christmas Lauds

In Leipzig, it was customary during Christmas to introduce into the Latin text of the Magnificat four Lauds – hymns in Latin and German – a practice which the civic authorities had tried unsuccessfully to stop in 1702[3]. These Lauds had featured in Kuhnau's settings, as evident in a set of parts still extant in Leipzig[4]. Bach sets the same texts, in the same order as Kuhnau:

> **A** a setting of Martin Luther's chorale 'Vom Himmel hoch'
>
> **B** 'Freut euch und jubiliert', an anonymous text derived from Luke ii, 10
>
> **C** a text derived from the greater doxology 'Gloria in excelsis Deo'
>
> **D** a verse from 'Virga Jesse', a Christmas hymn dating from the late sixteenth century

However, the fact that they are grouped together at the back of the manuscript, with indications in the score as to where they should be placed, seems to indicate that they were not originally planned as part of the work, but added as an afterthought. Whether this was as a result of Bach learning at a late stage of composition that he had to follow the precedent established by Kuhnau and his predecessors, abandoning an early plan to use material already written by Kuhnau, or considering these movements to be optional, we shall not know for certain. But Marshall (op. cit.) describes how, far from being composed in the same style as the rest of *Magnificat*, these interpolations seem to survey a range of previous historical styles of vocal music. 'Vom Himmel hoch' is a cantus-firmus motet in the strict *stile antico*. 'Freut euch und jubiliert' is polyphonic, with an independent basso continuo and pairs of voices moving in parallel motion that recalls the motets of Monteverdi, or an earlier setting of the same text (1603) by Sethus Calvisius - himself a Thomaskantor in Leipzig in the early seventeenth century. 'Gloria in excelsis Deo', with its violin obbligato, proceeds in a homophonic fashion reminiscent of Carissimi's later Italian style, as cultivated by the Thomaskantors Johann Schelle, Kuhnau, and others. 'Virga Jesse', by contrast, is the most contemporary in style, being written as a florid operatic duet for soprano and bass soloists with continuo. This last movement introduces the only problem in providing a new performing edition of BWV243a, since the last page of the MS is missing, leaving 'Virga Jesse' incomplete at bar 30 (see below).

Magnificat in E flat was published by N. Simrock (Bonn) in 1811 as *Magnificat a cinque voci* – with one hand (C) added at the end – but omitted from the Bachgesellschaft edition (Leipzig, 1851-99). It appeared in the Neue Ausgabe (NBA) in 1955. *Magnificat* in D was published in the Bachgesellschaft edition [11. Band Teil 1] in 1862, with the 4 Lauds from BWV243a (Laud D incomplete) added as an appendix/Anhang.

Magnificat in D (BWV 243)

Bach's revision was prepared sometime between 1728 and 1733 (possibly 1735)[5] and was most probably premiered on 2nd July 1733[6], when the Feast of the Visitation of Mary coincided with the end of national mourning for the death of the Elector of Saxony, Friedrich August I.

The two most obvious differences between the two versions are: the downward transposition into D major, which was a better key for the trumpets and drums and frequently used for such festal music (cf. movements in the *Christmas Oratorio* and B Minor Mass); and the augmentation of the orchestra by the introduction of a pair of flutes throughout (BWV243a only calls for two recorders or *flauti dolci* in movement No. 9.)

In the process of revision, Bach took the opportunity to make other changes. For example, compare No.8 bar 14, where the violins' upward flourish makes such a dramatic improvement to the line. For a passage where Bach's changes may not be such an improvement, compare No.4 bar 24, where the arresting dissonance of the dominant minor ninth has the sting taken out of it in the later version. No.10 is given an extra bar (bar 35) and has its obbligato scored for oboes rather than solo trumpet. This is such a practical alteration that it may have been occasioned by some memory of the movement not working well on the trumpet in 1723,

or because Gottfried Reiche (1667-1734), Bach's virtuoso trumpeter, was no longer available, and it could not be entrusted to any other player.

More importantly, by removing the four Christmas Lauds, Bach consolidated the work as one that could be used on those high feasts, (some fifteen in the Lutheran Church), when an elaborate setting of the Latin Magnificat was permitted.

Magnificat in D was revived by C.P.E. Bach for a performance in 1786 when he succeeded Telemann as director of music at the five principal churches in Hamburg.

EDITORIAL PROCEDURE
TEXT
The Latin text is the standard version of the Magnificat (taken from Luke i, 46-55) found in the Vulgate bible. Bach's only deviation from this text is his omission of the word 'eius' in the line 'Et misericordia eius a progenie in progenies timentibus eum' (No. 6) rendering its meaning as 'And [his] mercy is on them that fear him'. The fact that C.P.E. Bach sets the complete line in his *Magnificat* in D (1749), as does Schütz in his *Magnificat* SWV 468 (c.1665), seems to indicate that this was an oversight on the composer's part, rather than a customary change made in Lutheran worship.
MUSIC
The music of this edition is derived from the *Neuen Bach-Ausgabe* (1955/1959). Simrock and Bachgesellschaft edition of BWV243 [11. Band, Teil 1] were also consulted, as was Cantata 110 in the NBA to assist the completion of Laud D. Editorial dynamics, instructions and ornaments are shown in square brackets, editorial ties and slurs are shown as 'cut' ties and 'cut' slurs (that is with a stroke through the tie or slur). The editorial continuo realisation is shown in small sized notes.
COMPLETION OF LAUD D
For the completion of the missing portion of 'Virga Jesse', the editor is indebted to Alfred Dürr's preface to his edition of BWV243a in the Bärenreiter Studienpartituren[7]. This reveals that the continuo part to the Duet 'Ehre sei Gott in der Höhe' (movement 5 of Cantata 110 for soprano and tenor soloists) is very nearly identical to the continuo part of this Laud – albeit in A rather than F . Consequently, tranposition of this material allows it to be used from bar 36 onwards to provide a suitable, and completely Bachian, ending. Since the last four bars are identical to the opening four bars, that leaves a mere eleven bars where the editor has had to reconstruct the vocal lines above it. This construction is based on the phrase-lengths and patterns of the vocal lines in corresponding passages of BWV110.

DYNAMICS

Bach used dynamics sparingly in BWV243 and not at all in BWV243a. In some places they indicate the difference between an orchestral ritornello and an accompanying passage (for example No.2 bars 17, 21, 51, No. 6 bar 32 etc.) These have been incorporated in BWV243a as editorial dynamics. A limited number of editorial dynamics have been added to both versions where they will be of assistance.

APPOGGIATURAS

Editorial appoggiaturas have been added where they are missing from a repeat (for example No. 8 at bar 65).

THE REHEARSAL PIANO ACCOMPANIMENT

I have provided a new rehearsal accompaniment, in which the material based on instrumental parts is in full sized type and editorial realisation is in cue-size. I have tried represent all of the orchestration, although it has not been possible to preserve every part at the correct pitch.

THE ORCHESTRAL SCORE AND PARTS

The score and parts, available on hire from the publisher, are newly engraved and correspond exactly with this vocal score. The orchestral parts may be used for either period or modern instrument performances. A newly-arranged Continuo Keyboard part is suitable for chamber organ or harpsichord.

Trumpets and Timpani BWV243 requires 3 D trumpets; BWV243a - 3 E flat trumpets.

three virtuoso players are required, with Trumpet 1 needing to reach d''' (e♭''' in BWV243a). The timpani are tuned to D & A (E flat & B flat in BWV243a).

Flutes There are two parts for flutes in BWV243. The only movement for flutes in BWV243a is No. 9, which is designated for two recorders (*flauto dolce*). There is, however, no reason why this may not also be played on the *flauto traverso*, since Simrock (1811) designates them as '2 flauti'.

Oboes In BWV243 Bach's requirements are for two players doubling oboes and oboe d'amore. Transpositions of the d'amore music (Nos. 3 & 4) are given in an appendix, thus allowing the whole piece to be played on 2 oboes if so desired. BWV243a needs two oboes only. The oboe parts to BWV243a also contain the trumpet obbligato for No.10 in case it is felt that an oboe obbligato would be more appropriate here (as in BWV243.)

Strings The string parts contain all the bowing and articulation found in the MS of BWV243. (BWV243a has none). The bowing and articulation of BWV243 has been carried over into BWV243a, and is shown there in square brackets or by cut-slurs. Care has

been taken over the positioning of page-turns. The differences between the two versions of the work for strings are:

BWV243a		BWV243
No. 6	strings	muted strings and 2 flutes
No. 8	violins I, II and viola	violins I and II
No. 9	not designated pizzicato	continuo cello pizzicato
No.10*	violins I, II and viola	cello, senza violone

*This movement contains one note which is too low for the violin, but this music is cued in the cello part.

N.B. In BWV243a the cello continuo is needed for Lauds B, C, and D; and violin I plays in C.

Keyboard Continuo This is the part from which the continuo should be played. The vocal score is no adequate substitute since it is a piano reduction for rehearsal purposes. The keyboard continuo part contains the few figured bass markings found in the MS, and a new realisation which will be of enormous assistance to those not used to improvising from an unfigured bass line.

ACKNOWLEDGEMENTS

Thanks are due to Hywel Davies for his help in seeing this through to publication.

Neil Jenkins
Hove
February 2000

1 R. L. Marshall: *On the origin of the Magnificat, The Music of Johann Sebastian Bach* (New York: Schirmer, 1989)

2 C. S. Terry: *Bach: The Magnificat, Lutheran Masses and Motets* (London, 1929)

3 M. Geck: 'J.S. Bach's Weihnachts-Magnificat und sein Traditionszusammenhang', *Musik und Kirche* xxxi (1961)

4 Musikbibliothek der Stadt Leipzig, Sammlung Becker III.2.124.

5 M. Boyd: 'Bach', J.M. Dent *The Master Musicians* (London, 1983)

6 S. Heighes: 'Magnificat' in *J.S. Bach: Oxford Composer Companions* ed. M. Boyd, (Oxford, 1999)

7 A. Dürr: Preface to *J.S. Bach: Magnificat, Bärenreiter Studienpartitur 58*, (Kassel, 1959), pp. iv, vi,

NOTE

The Novello edition of *Magnificat* in D (NOV07033), which this edition supersedes, was published in 1874 with an English translation by the Reverend John Troutbeck (1832-99), loosely based on the text found in The Book of Common Prayer. The present edition presents both versions of the work, with a new piano accompaniment and with all editorial realisations and interventions clearly shown. The only English translations provided are those for the Christmas Lauds.

The present edition of the *Magnificat* in D follows the layout of NOV07033 (except for page 36) to allow the two editions to be used side by side.

MAGNIFICAT in D

1 **[CHORUS]**

[Tpts., Timp., Fls., Obs., Stgs., Cont. Org.]

2

Chorus

2 **[ARIA]**

SOPRANO 2 SOLO

Et ex - sul - ta - vit spi - ri - tus_ me - us,

Et ex - sul - ta - vit spi - ri - tus_ me - us,

et ex - sul - ta - vit spi - ri - tus__ me - us, et ex - sul -

-ta - - - - - - - vit__ spi - ri - tus__ me -

-us in De - - o sa - lu - ta - - ri, sa - lu -

-ta - - - - - - - - - - - - -

3 **[ARIA]**

Adagio

4 **[CHORUS]**

18

20

generation | ge-ne-ra-ti-o-nes, | omnes, om-nes ge-ne-ra-ti-o-nes.
ge-ne-ra-ti-o-nes, | om - nes ge-ne-ra-ti-o-nes.
ge-ne-ra-ti-o-nes, | om - nes ge-ne-ra-ti-o-nes.
ge-ne-ra-ti-o-nes, | om - nes_ ge - ne - ra-ti-o-nes.
om nes, om-nes ge - ne - ra - ti - o - - - - - nes.

5 **[ARIA]**

[Cont. Org.]

BASS SOLO

Qui-a fe-cit_ mi-hi mag-na,

24

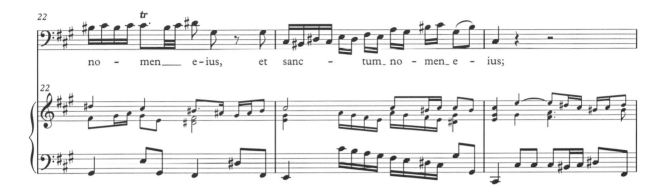

6 [DUET]

ALTO SOLO [p]

Et mi-se-ri-cor-di-a,_____ mi-se-ri-cor-di-a_____ a pro-ge-

TENOR SOLO [p]

Et mi-se-ri-cor-di-a,_____ mi-se-ri-cor-di-a_____ a pro-ge-ni-e

[Fls., Stgs., Cont. Org.]

-ni-e in_____ pro-ge-ni-es;

in__ pro-ge-ni-es, in__ pro-ge-ni-es;

e – um, ti-men – ti-bus, ti-men – – – ti-bus, ti-

e – um, ti-men – ti-bus, ti-men – – – ti-bus, ti-

-men-ti-bus e – um, ti-men – – – ti-bus e – um.

-men-ti-bus e – um, ti-men – – – ti-bus e – um.

[mf]

7 [CHORUS]

34

8 **[ARIA]**

[Vlns., Cont. Org.]

TENOR SOLO

De - po - - su - it, de-

38

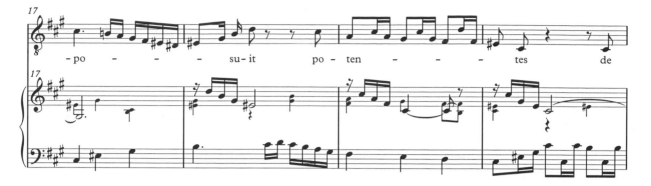

et ex-al-ta - - - -

- vit hu - mi - les.

9 [ARIA]

[Fls., Cont. Org.]

ALTO SOLO

E - su - ri - en - tes im - ple — vit bo - nis,

e - su - ri - en - tes im - ple — vit bo - nis et di - vi - tes_ di - mi - sit, et

di - vi - tes_ di - mi - sit, di - mi - sit in - a - nes, et di - vi - tes_ di - mi - sit in-

-a - nes, di - mi - sit in - a - nes.

E - su - ri - en - tes im-

-ple - vit_ bo - nis, e - su - ri - en - tes im - ple - vit bo - -

nis, im - ple - - -

- - - - - - - - - vit_

bo - nis et di - vi - tes_ di - mi - sit, et di - vi - tes_ di - mi - sit, di - mi - sit

in - a - nes, di - mi - sit in - a - nes, di - mi - sit in - a - nes.

10 **[TRIO]**

SOPRANO 1 [Solo or semi-chorus]
Su - sce - pit_ Is - ra-el pu - e - rum_ su - um, su-sce - pit_

SOPRANO 2 [Solo or semi-chorus]
Su - sce - pit_ Is - ra-el pu - e - rum_

ALTO [Solo or semi-chorus]
Su - sce - pit_ Is - ra-el pu - e - rum_ su - um,

[Obs., Cont. Org.]

Is - ra-el, su-sce - pit_ Is - ra-el, su-sce - pit_ Is - ra-el,

su - um, su-sce - pit_ Is - ra-el, su - sce - pit_

su-sce - pit_ Is - ra-el, su - sce - pit_ Is - ra-el pu - e - rum_

45

46

11 [CHORUS]

50

52

- la, A - bra-ham et se-mi-ni e - ius in sae - cu - la.

- la, A - bra-ham et___ se-mi-ni e - ius in sae - cu - la.

- la, A - bra-ham et se-mi-ni e - ius in sae - cu - la.

- la, A - bra-ham et se-mi-ni e - ius in sae - cu - la.

-stros, A - bra-ham et se - mi-ni e - ius___ in sae - cu - la.

12 [CHORUS]

Glo - ri - a,

Glo - ri - a, glo -

Glo - ri - a, glo - - - -

Glo - ri - a, glo - - - - -

Glo - ri - a, glo - - - - - -

[Tpts., Timp.
Fls., Obs., Stgs.,
Cont. Org.]

56

58

Magnificat in E flat

(BWV243a)

MAGNIFICAT in E flat

1 [CHORUS]

[*f*]

[Tpts., Timp.,
Obs., Stgs.,
Cont. Org.]

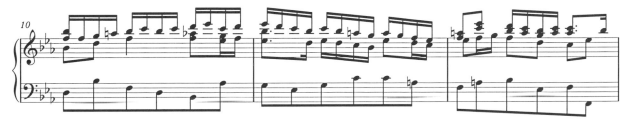

63

69

70

2 [ARIA]

SOPRANO 2 SOLO

Et ex-sul - ta – vit spi – ri – tus_ me - us,

et ex-sul - ta – vit spi – ri – tus_ me - us,

-ri__ me-o,__ in De-o__ sa-lu - ta - - ri me - o;

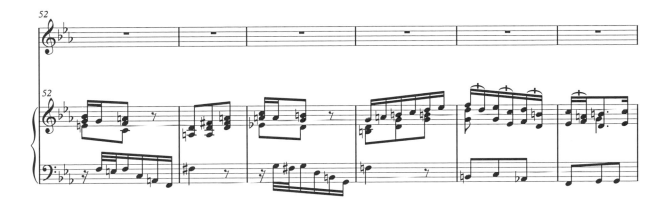

et ex-sul-ta - vit spi-ri-tus_ me - us in De -

-o sa-lu - ta - - ri, sa-lu - ta - - -

[A. 1st Christmas Laud]

3 **[ARIA]**

[Adagio]

SOPRANO 1 SOLO

Qui - a__ re - spe - xit

hu - mi - li - ta - tem, hu - mi - li - ta - tem an - cil - lae su - ae,

qui - a__ re - spe - xit hu - mi - li - ta - tem,

hu - mi - li - ta - tem an - cil - lae su - ae:

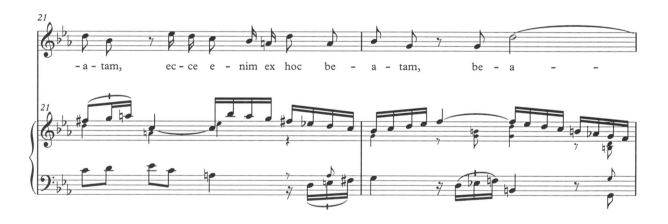

4 [CHORUS]

84

* no accidentals are given in the MS: this phrase corresponds with the same passage in the D major setting

ge - ne - ra - ti - o - nes, om - nes, om - nes ge - ne - ra - ti - o - nes.

ge - ne - ra - ti - o - nes, om - nes ge - ne - ra - ti - o - nes.

ge - ne - ra - ti - o - nes, om - nes ge - ne - ra - ti - o - nes.

ge - ne - ra - ti - o - nes, om - nes ge - ne - ra - ti - o - nes.

om - nes, om - nes ge - ne - ra - ti - o - nes.

5 **[ARIA]**

[Cont. Org.]

BASS SOLO

Qui - a fe - cit mi - hi mag - na,

92

[B. 2nd Christmas Laud]

Chorus [or Semi-chorus]

94

e - um, ti - men - ti-bus, ti - men - - ti-bus, ti-

e - um, ti - men - ti-bus, ti - men - - ti-bus, ti-

-men-ti-bus e - um, ti - men - - ti-bus e - um.

-men-ti-bus e - um, ti - men - ti-bus e - um.

[mf]

7 [CHORUS]

* In the D major version this note is the same as the note for the Basses, although no accidental is given in the E♭ version

102

* In the D major version this note is the same as the note for the Basses, although no accidental is given in the E♭ version

* In the D major version this note is the same as the note for the orchestral Bass, although no accidental is given in the E♭ version

* This note is given as A♮ in Urtext, and therefore breaks the pattern set in bars, 1,5,9 and 13. In the D major version, however, it still agrees with the bass note.

108

[C. 3rd Christmas Laud]

Chorus

112

8 **[ARIA]**

[Vln., Vla.,
Cont. Org.]

TENOR SOLO

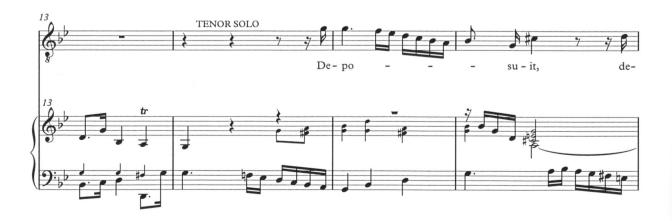

De- po - - su- it, de-

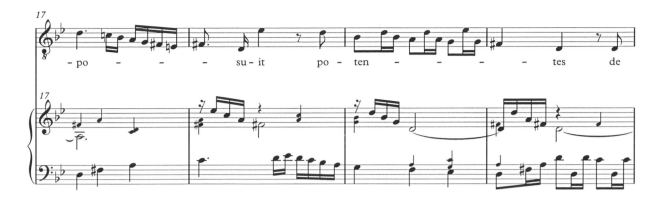

-po — — — su - it po - ten — — - tes de

se — — — de et ex - al - ta — —

- — — — — — vit hu - mi - les;

de- po — — — su it, de-

-po — — — su-it po - ten — — tes de

se — — de et ex-al - ta — — — —

— — — vit, et ex - al - ta - vit hu - mi — les,_____

115

et ex-al-ta - - - -

- vit hu - mi - les.

116

9 [ARIA]

ALTO SOLO

E - su - ri - en - tes im - ple - vit bo nis,

e - su - ri - en - tes im - ple - vit bo - nis et di - vi - tes_ di - mi - sit, et

[D. 4th Christmas Laud]

[Cont. Org.]

SOPRANO SOLO

Vir – ga Jes – se flo – – – – – – – – – – – –
Jes – se's stem is flo – – – – – – – – – – – –

BASS SOLO

Vir – ga Jes – se flo – – – – – –
Jes – se's stem is flo – – – – – –

* Editorial reconstruction from here to end of movement (see Preface)

124

10 **[TRIO]**

11 **[CHORUS]**

Chorus

134

- la, A - bra-ham et se - mi-ni e — ius in sae - cu - la.

- la, A - bra-ham et___ se - mi-ni e — ius in sae - cu - la.

- la, A - bra-ham et se - mi-ni e — ius in sae - cu - la.

- la, A - bra-ham et se - mi-ni e — ius in sae - cu - la.

-stros, A - bra-ham et se - mi-ni e — ius___ in sae - cu - la.

12 **[CHORUS]**

Chorus

SOPRANO 1 [*f*]

Glo - ri - a,

SOPRANO 2 [*f*]

Glo - ri - a, glo -

ALTO [*f*]

Glo - ri - a, glo - - -

TENOR [*f*]

Glo - ri - a, glo - - -

BASS [*f*]

Glo - ri - a, glo - -

[*f*]

[Tpts., Timp.
Obs., Stgs.
Cont. Org.]

140

Printed and bound in Great Britain by Caligraving Limited